WOULD YOU RATHER?

200 SUPER SILLY, FUN QUESTIONS, HILARIOUS SCENARIOS AND WACKY CHOICES FOR EXCITING GAME TIME WITH FAMILY AND FRIENDS

Are you ready to have some wacky conversations?

Welcome to the ultimate collection of extra-silly, super-fun, and wildly creative questions for the most hilarious Easter game time!

Perfect for family, friends, and anyone looking to add some laughter and excitement to your Easter celebration!

Whether you're hanging out at home, enjoying a playdate, celebrating in class, giggling through a sleepover, or speding time with loved ones, this game is your ticket to unforgettable fun!

Get ready for wild imagination and lots of laughing!

HOW TO PLAY

 You'll need 2 players or more.
4 WAYS TO PLAY!

Just For Fun: (no scoring)

1. Decide who goes first.
2. Player 1 chooses and reads a question for the next player (Player 2) to answer.
3. Player 2 answers the question by selecting one of the two answer choices.
4. The player that just answered becomes the next player to ask a question—either back to Player 1 (if there are only two players) or to the next player in the circle.

(You can only choose ONE answer!)

You can also ask the person to explain why they chose their answer. This part can add a lot of fun and is a cool way to learn more about each other!

MORE WAYS TO PLAY

Optional ways to play by scoring:

2 Made You Laugh Challenge:

Try to make the other players laugh as you explain why you chose your answer. Get a point each time anyone laughs. At the end, tally up to see who made the most laughs.

3 Guess My Answer:

The player answering the question silently chooses an answer. The other players try to guess which answer was chosen.
Once the correct answer is revealed, the players who guessed right will each get a point. Tally up the points to see who was the best guesser with the most points.

4 Everyone Answers:

Here, one player asks the question to everyone else. Each person gets a chance to explain their answer. The player who read out the question will decide who gave the best answer. The player with the best answers will get a point. The next player asks the next question.

WOULD YOU RATHER ....

Have an Easter egg that hatches into a unicorn

———— OR ————

into a baby dragon?

Have a pet bunny that grants wishes

————————

a magic Easter egg that finishes your homework?

WOULD YOU RATHER ....

Get grandma's
homemade candy

—————— OR ——————

high-tech candy
from the future?

Play hopscotch
with a bunny

—————— OR ——————

play video games
with a baby chick?

WOULD YOU RATHER ....

Swim in a pool of melted chocolate

OR

a sea of jellybeans?

Search for eggs in a coral reef

OR

dive for jellybeans in a sunken ship?

WOULD YOU RATHER ....

Live in a giant
Easter egg house

OR

in a carrot
shaped treehouse?

Have a bunny that
can talk

OR

chicks that
can dance?

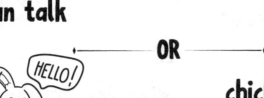

HELLO!

WOULD YOU RATHER ....

Paint Easter eggs
with your toes

OR

eat a chocolate
bunny with no hands?

Have chocolate
syrup for hair

OR

jellybean teeth?

WOULD YOU RATHER ....

Eat your lunch
with bunny paws

— OR —

drink water with a
chick's beak?

Have a teacher who's
a dancing bunny

— OR —

a teacher who
only speaks in jokes?

WOULD YOU RATHER ....

Wear an Easter egg costume all day

—— OR ——

a bunny suit with a fluffy tail?

Have Easter every month

—— OR ——

have your birthday twice a year?

WOULD YOU RATHER ....

Juggle chocolate
Easter eggs

———— OR ————

ride a unicycle while
eating jellybeans?

Watch a lion do
an Easter egg hunt

———— OR ————

see an elephant
paint Easter eggs?

WOULD YOU RATHER ....

Get a golden egg
full of sour candy

——— OR ———

one full of
mashed potatoes?

Eat only Easter
candy forever

——— OR ———

never eat Easter
candy again?

9

WOULD YOU RATHER ....

An Easter scavenger
hunt with clues

OR

a giant Easter
egg piñata?

Climb a giant
chocolate bunny

OR

slide down an
Easter egg mountain?

WOULD YOU RATHER ....

A bunny that tells
silly jokes

•————— OR —————•

HA-HA!

a chick that
whispers secrets?

Have to sleep in a
giant Easter basket

•————— OR —————•

a bed made of
cotton candy?

WOULD YOU RATHER ....

Have a book of
Easter spells

———— OR ————

a map that leads to a
hidden land of candy?

Be able to make
chocolate eggs float

———— OR ————

make jellybeans
dance?

WOULD YOU RATHER ....

Have to find
1,000 eggs

———— **OR** ————

hide **1,000** eggs
for others?

Race a speeding
bunny

———— **OR** ————

catch a flying
gummy bear?

WOULD YOU RATHER ....

Eat jelly beans for breakfast

——— OR ———

chocolate eggs for dinner?

Hop everywhere for a week

——— OR ———

say "Happy Easter" after every sentence?

WOULD YOU RATHER ....

An Easter egg that glows in the dark

OR

one that can float in the air?

Wear bunny slippers

OR

a carrot hat all day?

WOULD YOU RATHER ....

Have a bunny that
never stops hopping

OR

a chick that never
stops chirping?

Own a cow that makes
endless chocolate milk

OR

a chicken that lays
perfectly fried eggs?

WOULD YOU RATHER ....

A cape that makes you fly

OR

gloves that shoot chocolate syrup?

Be able to turn any food into jellybeans

OR

make carrots taste like pizza?

WOULD YOU RATHER ....

Slide down a
gummy rainbow

——— OR ———

ride on a giant
bunny's back?

Have a magic wand
that makes candy

——— OR ———

an Easter basket
that never empties?

WOULD YOU RATHER ....

Have to wear bunny ears on picture day

—— OR ——

a clown costume for show-and-tell?

A bunny that helps with your homework

—— OR ——

a chick that gives test answers?

WOULD YOU RATHER ....

Have a cotton candy
cloud follow you

———— OR ————

a popcorn machine that
pops out jellybeans?

Ride a dragon made
of chocolate

———— OR ————

ride a marshmallow
unicorn?

WOULD YOU RATHER ....

Play soccer with a
bouncy chocolate egg

OR

basketball with a
giant jellybean?

Have a skateboard with
Easter egg wheels

OR

rollerblades that
spray chocolate?

WOULD YOU RATHER ....

Collect eggs guarded
by a grumpy troll

——— OR ———

by a young
werewolf?

Have a pet Peep that
lays mini marshmallows

——— OR ———

a pet chocolate bunny
that never melts?

WOULD YOU RATHER ....

Do an egg hunt with a knight in shining armor

OR

with a ninja from Japan?

Get your Easter basket from a pirate ship

OR

from an alien spaceship?

WOULD YOU RATHER ....

Wear socks filled with melted chocolate

———— **OR** ————

gloves made of sticky taffy?

Eat a 1,000-year-old chocolate bunny

———— **OR** ————

a jellybean that changes flavors every second?

WOULD YOU RATHER ....

Get caught in a
jellybean storm

— OR —

a chocolate
rain shower?

Fly a candy-powered
rocket

— OR —

dive in a gummy
submarine?

WOULD YOU RATHER ....

Decorate 100 Easter eggs by yourself

——— OR ———

eat 100 jelly beans in one sitting?

Have to dip everything you eat in chocolate

——— OR ———

sprinkle crushed Peeps on all your food?

26

WOULD YOU RATHER ....

Have an octopus that paints eggs

OR

a dolphin that delivers candy?

Have a bunny that swims like a fish

OR

a fish that hops like a bunny?

WOULD YOU RATHER ....

Have a pet bunny that can time travel

— OR —

a pet chick that tells the future?

Do an egg hunt in Ancient Egypt pyramids

— OR —

in the Wild West with cowboy bunnies?

WOULD YOU RATHER ....

Fight a slimey
chocolate monster

OR

battle a fluffy
giant chick?

Have a bunny sidekick
in a game

OR

a pet chicken that
lays power-ups?

WOULD YOU RATHER ....

Wear an astronaut suit made of chocolate

OR

a helmet filled with jellybeans?

Find an Easter egg on the moon

OR

have an alien bunny as a pet?

WOULD YOU RATHER ....

Eat a marshmallow as big as your head

——— OR ———

a chocolate egg as big as your bed?

Have to feed jellybeans to a zombie

——— OR ———

make a vampire drink carrot juice?

WOULD YOU
RATHER ....

Use fruit roll-ups
as a ruler

———— OR ————

use a chocolate
bar as a pencil?

Have a lunchbox that
refills with Peeps

———— OR ————

a bottle that pours
endless chocolate milk?

WOULD YOU RATHER ....

Have a bunny that
snores like a bear

———— OR ————

a duck that
quacks in its sleep?

Have a bunny that lays
chocolate eggs

———— OR ————

a chick that lays
jellybeans?

WOULD YOU RATHER ....

Race a turtle for an
Easter egg

—— OR ——

do a three-legged race
with a giant bunny?

Play dodgeball with
Easter bunnies

—— OR ——

play soccer with
gummy bears?

WOULD YOU RATHER ....

Wake up covered
in feathers

——— OR ———

with a bunny on
your head?

Have an alien join
your egg hunt

HAHA!

——— OR ———

meet a space bunny that
tells cosmic jokes?

WOULD YOU RATHER ....

An Easter egg that
turns into a dinosaur

——— OR ———

one that hatches a
tiny robot?

Get an Easter gift from
an ancient caveman

——— OR ———

one from a scientist
in the future?

WOULD YOU RATHER ....

Take a math test where
numbers are jellybeans

———— OR ————

an art test where you
paint with chocolate?

Have a class pet that's
a playful bunny

———— OR ————

a cute sleepy
baby chick?

WOULD YOU RATHER ....

Eat a chocolate bunny filled with ketchup

— OR —

a marshmallow dipped in mustard?

Drink a potion that turns you into a bunny

— OR —

eat a carrot that makes you hop like a bunny?

WOULD YOU RATHER ....

Chase a runaway egg down a hill

— OR —

 try to catch flying jellybeans in the wind?

Build a fort out of Easter baskets

— OR —

a castle out of Easter eggs?

WOULD YOU RATHER ....

Run a race against
a giant Peep

——— OR ———

hide from a bunny
on roller skates?

Go on an Easter egg
hunt in a giant maze

——— OR ———

in a spooky
chocolate house?

WOULD YOU RATHER ....

Find one long chocolate bar in your pocket

— OR —

always find a jellybean in your shoe?

A wand that paints Easter eggs with a flick

— OR —

one that makes candy appear out of thin air?

WOULD YOU RATHER ....

Have recess in a giant Easter basket

— OR —

in a field of chocolate flowers?

Use crayons that color like melted chocolate

— OR —

pencils that leave behind jellybean trails?

WOULD YOU RATHER ....

Eat a Peep that
screams when biten

—— OR ——

a chocolate bunny
that runs away?

Play hide and seek
with bunnies

—— OR ——

have a race with
laughing chicks?

WOULD YOU RATHER ....

Have a trampoline made of marshmallows

—— OR ——

a seesaw made of chocolate bars?

Have a bunny that can do flips

—— OR ——

a chick that can jump through a hoop?

WOULD YOU RATHER ....

Drink a smoothie made of jellybeans

—— OR ——

a milkshake made of melted chocolate bunnies?

Have an Easter egg made of cheese

—— OR ——

one made of ice cream?

WOULD YOU RATHER ....

Have a teacher who only speaks in cat noises

— OR —

 one who hands out tests written on Easter eggs?

Sit on tomato shaped chairs

— OR —

 use giant carrot pencils?

WOULD YOU RATHER ....

A class where every lesson is about chocolate

OR

one where every subject is taught by a bunny?

Have a lunchbox full of candy carrots

OR

a backpack that's an Easter egg?

47

WOULD YOU RATHER ....

Meet an alien that looks like a giant Peep

———— OR ————

a bunny that talks in beeps and boops?

Have a chocolate meteor land in your backyard

———— OR ————

a giant Peep spaceship parked on your roof?

WOULD YOU RATHER ....

Visit an underwater
cave filled with candy

—— OR ——

a coral reef
that sings?

Play with sea turtles
that bounce like bunnies

—— OR ——

starfish that giggle
like Peeps?

WOULD YOU RATHER ....

Live in a bunny's burrow

—— OR ——

a chicken's coop?

Find the most chocolate eggs ever

—— OR ——

the biggest chocolate egg in the world?

WOULD YOU RATHER ....

Have cotton candy
that lasts forever

—— OR ——

a sword that turns
things into chocolate?

Be able to turn water
into carrot juice

—— OR ——

make anything
bounce like a bunny?

51

WOULD YOU RATHER ....

Steal a chocolate fountain

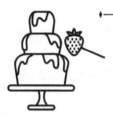

OR

steal golden eggs?

Have a space bunny that farts glitter

OR

an alien chick that speaks in riddles?

WOULD YOU RATHER ....

Wake up with bunny ears that wiggle

—— OR ——

bunny wiskers that tickle?

Eat a Peep that smells like feet

—— OR ——

a jellybean that tastes like soap?

WOULD YOU RATHER ....

Have an Easter egg
that teleports you

——— OR ———

one that can make
you invisible?

Make carrots taste
like candy

——— OR ———

make candy as
healthy as carrots?

WOULD YOU RATHER ....

Have to perform a silly
bunny dance

———— OR ————

tell jokes dressed
as a pig?

Be shot out of a cannon
into a marshmallow pit

———— OR ————

jump into a giant
jellybean trampoline?

WOULD YOU RATHER ....

Eat jellybeans that make you burp rainbows

————— OR —————

chocolate that makes you talk like a robot?

A chocolate bunny melt every time you touch it

————— OR —————

a marshmallow Peep that never stops growing?

WOULD YOU RATHER ....

Eat candy that
makes you glow

—— OR ——

jellybeans that
make you float?

A cafeteria that serves
only chocolate for lunch

—— OR ——

one that serves only
bunny-shaped donuts?

WOULD YOU RATHER ....

Meet an alien
Easter Bunny

—— OR ——

a robot that paints
eggs at super speed?

Ride on a cotton
candy storm cloud

—— OR ——

in an egg-shaped
spaceship?

WOULD YOU RATHER ....

Have a pillow stuffed with marshmallow fluff

OR

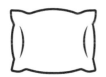

a blanket made of fruit roll-ups?

Find an Easter egg filled with monster slime

OR

one that hatches a baby Frankenstein?

WOULD YOU RATHER ....

A desk that hops
like a bunny

———— OR ————

spins in crazy circles?

Have a talking chocolate
bunny as your gym coach

———— OR ————

Run!

a grumpy marshmallow
Peep as your principal?

WOULD YOU RATHER ....

Go on an adventure with a pirate chick

—— **OR** ——

relax on a beach with a ninja chicken?

Have a tree that grows chocolate eggs

—— **OR** ——

a bush that pops out candy?

WOULD YOU RATHER ....

Have a pet fish that wears bunny ears

—— OR ——

a pet seahorse that wears a bunny tail?

A mermaid friend who loves chocolate

—— OR ——

a merman who collects Easter eggs?

WOULD YOU RATHER ....

Be chased by a
chocolate gorilla

—— OR ——

a marshmallow
polar bear?

Shoot jellybeans from
a candy gun

—— OR ——

throw chocolate coins
like ninja stars?

WOULD YOU RATHER ....

Write about the Easter Bunny's secret life

---- OR ----

draw a picture of a magical Easter land?

An Easter egg that tells bad jokes

---- OR ----

one that sings silly songs?

WOULD YOU RATHER ....

Race a spaceship that runs on jellybeans

—— OR ——

a bunny driving a carrot car?

Have an egg hunt in space

—— OR ——

a chocolate feast on the moon?

WOULD YOU RATHER ....

Eat popcorn that tastes like chocolate

—— OR ——

 hot chocolate that tastes like popcorn?

Have a fridge that only makes Easter candy

—— OR ——

 a backpack that refills with carrots?

WOULD YOU RATHER ....

Hop like a bunny every time someone says 'Easter'

—— OR ——

 meow like a cat all day?

Have a talking dog as your best friend

—— OR ——

 a magical cat that can grant one wish a day?

WOULD YOU RATHER ....

A rocket ship shaped like a giant Peep

—— OR ——

a moon made of chocolate chips?

Discover a new planet made of Easter candy

—— OR ——

one where bunnies rule the world?

WOULD YOU RATHER ....

Get turned into a
chocolate statue

——— OR ———

into a bouncing
marshmallow?

Have a backpack that
randomly drops jellybeans

——— OR ———

one that smells like a
hard-boiled egg?

WOULD YOU RATHER ....

Find an egg filled
with gold

OR

one that explodes
with confetti?

Zap stuff with
power lasers

OR

melt away problems
with special magic?

WOULD YOU RATHER ....

Have a library filled
with gummy books

— OR —

a cafeteria that
serves egg pizzas?

Have a pencil that walks
away if you forget it

— OR —

an eraser that
giggles when used?

WOULD YOU RATHER ....

Wear bunny tails that make you float

———— OR ————

a magic hat that turns what you touch into candy?

A magic jellybean that makes you super tall

———— OR ————

a chocolate bar that lets you shrink?

WOULD YOU RATHER ....

Train a bunny to
do circus tricks

———— OR ————

have a chick that can
ride a tiny bicycle?

Ride an elephant that
lays giant Easter eggs

———— OR ————

have chocolate
roller skates?

WOULD YOU RATHER ....

Hunt for Easter eggs
on the Moon

OR

chocolate carrots
on **Mars**?

Discover a planet
made of jellybeans

OR

one made of
chocolate?

WOULD YOU RATHER ....

Play underwater tag
with a talking fish

—— OR ——

Tag!

hide eggs in a
giant shipwreck?

Have coral that
grows candy

—— OR ——

seaweed that smells
like carrot cake?

WOULD YOU RATHER ....

Have a bunny tail that wiggles when you laugh

—— OR ——

duck feet that slap loudly when you walk?

Cluck like a chicken when someone says your name

—— OR ——

hop like a bunny every time you hear music?

WOULD YOU RATHER ....

Have a pet duck that lays golden eggs

OR

a bunny that hides candy?

Have an Easter egg that glows

OR

one that bounces?

WOULD YOU RATHER ....

Have to jump over **100** Easter eggs

OR

run through a field of giant jellybeans?

Find a hidden treasure chest full of candy

OR

one full of magical carrots?

WOULD YOU RATHER ....

Have a pet bunny
that can juggle

———— OR ————

a pet chick that can
walk on a tightrope?

Be a clown who throws
candy instead of pies

———— OR ————

a magician who pulls
Easter eggs out of hats?

WOULD YOU RATHER ....

Find Easter eggs
hidden in a pyramid

OR

in an underwater
lost city?

Hide Easter eggs in a
dinosaur jungle

OR

in a sand castle
full of knights?

WOULD YOU RATHER ....

Have to eat a three-foot-tall Peep

OR

drink a gallon of jellybean juice?

Have spaghetti made of licorice

OR

mashed potatoes made of marshmallow?

WOULD YOU RATHER ....

Have underwater
eggs that bubble

OR

fish that chirp like
little chicks?

Find a treasure chest
filled with chocolate

OR

a net to catch
bouncing jellybeans?

WOULD YOU RATHER ....

Play baseball with a marshmallow Peep ball

— OR —

tennis with a carrot racket?

Get chased by a giant chocolate bunny

— OR —

a marshmallow monster?

WOULD YOU RATHER ....

Have a trophy that's a giant chocolate carrot

OR

a medal made of jellybeans?

Compete in a hopping contest

OR

an egg and spoon race?

WOULD YOU RATHER ....

Sleep in a cave filled with talking chocolate bats

—— OR ——

 singing gummy spiders?

Have a pet ghost bunny that appears and disappears

—— OR ——

 a skeleton chicken that breakdances?

WOULD YOU RATHER ....

Attend a picnic in a giant garden of carrots

—— OR ——

a secret Easter egg park?

Do homework that turns into a scavenger hunt

—— OR ——

tests that come with jellybean prizes?

WOULD YOU RATHER ....

Eat an Easter egg filled with spaghetti

———— OR ————

one filled with oatmeal?

Have pancakes topped with melted Peeps

———— OR ————

waffles with jellybean syrup?

WOULD YOU RATHER ....

Have to sleep in a
giant bird's nest

—— OR ——

live in a rabbit
hole for a day?

Have a pet duck that
follows you everywhere

—— OR ——

a pet bunny that
hides your socks?

88

WOULD YOU RATHER ....

Race against the Easter Bunny in an eating contest

———— OR ————

in a rolling-eggs-down-a-hill contest?

Eat jellybeans with chopsticks

———— OR ————

drink hot chocolate from a hose?

WOULD YOU RATHER ....

Be invisible whenever you wear bunny ears

—— OR ——

 be able to fly each time you chew a jellybean?

Have a giggle that makes chocolate rain

—— OR ——

 a secret code that makes candy carrots?

WOULD YOU RATHER ....

Explore an asteroid
belt of candy

———— OR ————

orbit around a moon
of marshmallow Peeps?

Float in space with a
carrot that talks to stars

———— OR ————

with an egg that
tells space jokes?

WOULD YOU RATHER ....

Design your own
Easter egg pattern

 — OR —

make a new Easter
candy flavor?

Invent a new
Easter game

— OR —

create a new Easter
tradition for your family?

WOULD YOU RATHER ....

Ride a broomstick that leaves a rainbow trail

— OR —

a flying Easter basket that shoots glitter?

See a magician show at your home

— OR —

see a chick transform into a butterfly?

WOULD YOU RATHER ....

Find an egg with an old treasure map inside

• ——— OR ——— •

one that opens a futuristic portal?

Teleport using a swirl of Easter colors

• ——— OR ——— •

transform into a giant?

WOULD YOU RATHER ....

Have laser vision that can toast Peeps

OR

make jellybeans explode like fireworks?

Be able to stretch like a spring

OR

be super strong when lifting baskets?

WOULD YOU RATHER ....

Explore a sunken pirate ship with candy treasure

—— OR ——

a castle made entirely of eggs?

Surf on a wave of melted chocolate

—— OR ——

dive into bouncing Easter eggs?

WOULD YOU RATHER ....

Bounce off walls like a rubber ball

———— OR ————

stick to surfaces like glue?

Have super hearing to listen for hidden eggs

———— OR ————

super sight to spot the tiniest candy?

WOULD YOU RATHER ....

Cast a spell that makes you run super fast

— OR —

one that lets you speak every animal language?

Have to solve a puzzle to get your Easter candy

— OR —

do a secret handshake?

WOULD YOU RATHER ....

Go camping in a giant
Easter basket

———— OR ————

ride in a
chocolate canoe?

Be able to shoot jellybeans
from your fingers

———— OR ————

sneeze chocolate sprinkles?

WOULD YOU RATHER ....

Be able to summon an army of tiny bunnies

—— OR ——

have a pet chick that grants three wishes?

Teleport to places with Easter eggs

—— OR ——

fly there while holding an umbrella?

THE END

Made in United States
Troutdale, OR
04/15/2025

30649663R20060